KINGS ✤ AND ✤ QUEENS

James VI/I

Faye Kalloniatis

Wayland

Titles in the series

Elizabeth I
Henry VIII
James VI/I
Mary Queen of Scots
Queen Victoria
William I

Series editor: Sarah Doughty
Book editor: Marcella Forster
Consultant: Kayte Wallace
Designer: Jean Wheeler
Production controller: Carol Stevens

First published in 1995 by Wayland (Publishers) Ltd
61 Western Road, Hove, East Sussex, BN3 1JD, England

British Library Cataloguing in Publication Data
Kalloniatis, Faye
King James VI/I – (Kings & Queens series)
I. Title II. Series
941.061092

ISBN 0 7502 1453 8

Typeset by Jean Wheeler
Printed and bound in Milan, Italy, by Rotolito Lombarda S.p.A.

Cover and frontispiece: Portraits of King James VI/I by John Decritz the Elder.

Picture acknowledgements
The publisher would like to thank the following for allowing their photographs and illustrations to be used in this book:
Bath Museums Service 22; Bridgeman Art Library *cover, frontispiece,* 7, 12, 13 (bottom), 17 (bottom), 20, 21 (bottom), 23 (left), 29; City of Edinburgh District Council 15 (bottom); Courtauld Institute of Art 23 (right); Mary Evans Picture Library 4 (bottom), 17 (top); Fotomas Index 21 (top); Robert Harding Picture Library 24; Hulton Deutsch Collection 11 (bottom), 13 (top), 15 (top), 18, 19 (top), 25 (both), 26, 28 (bottom); National Library of Scotland 16; National Portrait Gallery 9, 27, 28 (top); National Trust for Scotland 11 (top); Popperfoto 4 (top); The Royal Collection © 1995 Her Majesty the Queen 5; Scottish National Portrait Gallery 6 (both), 8 (both), 10, 14; Wayland Picture Library 19 (bottom).

Contents

The Boy King

In 1603 the people of England lined the streets, cheering the arrival of the man who was to be their new **monarch**. Some wrote poems to him, others prepared lavish banquets in his honour as he made the three-week journey to London from his home in Scotland.

But the man who was to be crowned King James I of England was no stranger to the throne. He was

(Above) The **Coronation** *Chair, in Westminster Abbey, on which James I was crowned King of England. It was specially built to hold the famous* **Stone of Scone** *under the seat.*

(Left) Lord Darnley and Mary Queen of Scots, James's parents.

already King James VI of Scotland – and had been since he was an infant.

James was born in Edinburgh Castle, Scotland, in 1566. His mother was the queen of Scotland – Mary Queen of Scots – and his father was the handsome Lord Darnley. Shortly after James's birth, Darnley was found dead in mysterious circumstances. Not long after that, his mother was forced to **abdicate** because she was very unpopular. James was next in line for the throne. He was taken to Stirling and crowned when he was only one year old.

Of course, James was far too young to govern his country, so **regents** were chosen to rule in his place until he was old enough to rule Scotland himself. Meanwhile, James spent the first thirteen years of his life at Stirling Castle in Scotland.

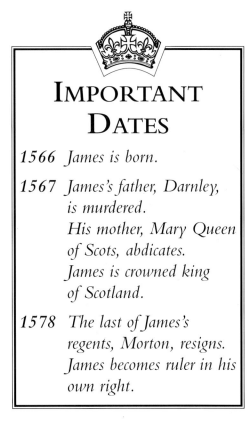

IMPORTANT DATES

1566 *James is born.*

1567 *James's father, Darnley, is murdered.*
His mother, Mary Queen of Scots, abdicates.
James is crowned king of Scotland.

1578 *The last of James's regents, Morton, resigns.*
James becomes ruler in his own right.

The infant James kneels in front of a statue of his dead father.

mistake
James'

(Above) George Buchanan,
James's senior tutor. He did not
like James's mother, Mary, and
often told the poor young king
what he thought of her.

James's childhood at Stirling Castle was an unhappy and friendless one. Much of his time was taken up with his education, which began when he was only four years old. His **tutor**, George Buchanan, made him work very hard. James was so frightened of him that he had nightmares about him.

James's lessons started very early in the day. First he studied Ancient Greek. Then, after breakfast, he worked on Latin and history. He was allowed a short lunch break, then had to continue his studies. In the afternoon he had a lesson in **composition**, followed by geography and then arithmetic. Only after all that was done was he allowed his supper.

(Right) Sir Peter Young, another
of James's tutors. He was very
kind to James and was later tutor
to one of James's own children.

Fortunately, James was a bright child and did well at his lessons. At the age of eight he could **translate** passages from the Bible from Latin into French, then into English. By the age of thirteen he had a library of six hundred books, believed to be the largest private collection in Scotland.

The young king's education could not have been better, but life at Stirling Castle was harsh. There were not many children to play with, and the adults did not know how to treat a young child. So James often felt lonely, unhappy and unloved.

A painting of Stirling in the time of James's reign. James was baptized in the castle, which can be seen on the right, and also spent his childhood there.

mistake James'

The regents **governed** Scotland for James until he was old enough to rule. By the time James was seven years old, he had already had four regents.

James had mixed feelings about his regents. He liked some, but he was unsure about others. The Earl of Lennox, James's grandfather, was his favourite regent. In 1571, when James was five, Lennox was murdered. His bleeding body was carried into the castle in front of the young boy. The horror of this stayed with James; he grew up hating violence and always wanting to make peace. This later earned him the title *beati pacifici*, which is Latin for 'a lover of the peace'.

The Earl of Moray, James's uncle and his first regent.

The last of James's regents was the Earl of Morton. He resigned unwillingly in 1578 and James became Scotland's head of government at twelve years old. Morton was later charged with being involved in the murder of James's father, Darnley, and was executed in 1581.

The Earl of Morton, James's last regent. He was a member of the powerful Douglas clan – a ruling family – and was executed for his part in the murder of James's father, Darnley.

James's childhood was not all bleak, though. He loved hunting and early portraits show him with hawks and falcons. Later, when James was an adult, he was criticized for spending too much time hunting and not enough governing his kingdom.

James at the age of eight. James loved to go hunting with falcons like the one perching on his hand.

A Scottish Ruler

Esmé Stuart, James's close friend, who later became the Duke of Lennox. Esmé's ruff collar was very fashionable at the time.

In 1579, when James was thirteen years old, a relative of his arrived from France. He was Esmé Stuart – a man old enough to be James's father. They quickly became friends and spent many happy hours together. Esmé, who was a **Catholic**, was even willing to change his religion and become a **Protestant** like James in order to please the young king.

The Scottish lords were jealous of this friendship. They were afraid Esmé had too much power over James. So in 1582 they 'kidnapped' James and held him at the House of Ruthven. Later, James's capture became known as the Raid of Ruthven. The lords urged James to send his friend Esmé back to France. At first James refused, but eventually he was forced to agree. Esmé departed, leaving James heartbroken. But James faced even greater sadness. In 1587 his mother, Mary, was found guilty of plotting to murder Queen Elizabeth I of England and was beheaded.

In 1600, when James was a young man, he fell victim to another plot. One day, while he was hunting near Falkland Palace, James was lured to Gowrie House. When he arrived, he was locked up. He only managed to escape by yelling out to his friends, who had come with him. In the struggle James's captors, the two Gowrie brothers, were killed. The Gowrie **Conspiracy** was never fully explained, but it increased James's fear of violence and made him even more determined to make peace.

Falkland Palace, which belonged to James. In 1592, three hundred men went to the palace to attack James but failed. James was locked in a tower for safety until the danger passed.

James (right) looks nervous as his men defend him during the Gowrie Conspiracy. The dead man on the ground is one of the two Gowrie brothers who were killed during the struggle.

Queen Anne, James's wife, at the age of nineteen.

In his early twenties, James decided to marry Princess Anne of Denmark. She was fourteen years old, and he had never met her. Arrangements were made for her to travel to Scotland by boat. But violent storms made it impossible for her to cross the North Sea. The terrified princess was tossed about in the ship and was nearly crushed to death by loose cannon. Eventually the ship was forced to land in Norway.

It was now James's turn to brave the storms and, fortunately, he had more luck than Anne. He reached Norway and met the young princess for the first time. They were married at once and spent several months in Scandinavia before preparing, yet again, to face the storms. This time they were successful and managed to land in Leith, Scotland, where a huge crowd had gathered to welcome them. Anne's journey from Leith to Edinburgh was spectacular; she travelled in a silver coach drawn by eight white horses.

IMPORTANT DATES

1579 *Esmé Stuart, a French relative of James, arrives in Scotland.*

1582 *Esmé returns to France and dies shortly afterwards.*

1587 *James's mother, Mary, is beheaded.*

1589 *James marries Princess Anne of Denmark.*

1594 *Prince Henry, James's first child, is born.*

1598 *James publishes* Trew Law of Free Monarchies, *a book about his belief in the* **divine right of kings**.

James interrogates the witches accused of raising a storm against his ship. At that time, people believed in witchcraft, and James even wrote a book about it.

When the couple were safely back, some people claimed the bad storms had been caused by witches. Several women were accused of witchcraft and were put on trial. James **interrogated** some of the accused. They were found guilty and were **executed.**

In Edinburgh, the king and queen settled down to married life. Their first child, Prince Henry, was born in 1594. Later, six more children were born, but they did not all reach adulthood.

James, wearing a jewel-encrusted outfit. It was fashionable to wear a cloak on one shoulder only.

IACOBVS · 6 · D · G · R ·
SCOTORVM ·
ÆTA · 29 ·
1595 ·

James as a young man.

Ruling Scotland was not an easy task, but James did well. Scotland was filled with lairds (Scottish lords) who belonged to different clans. James himself belonged to the Stuart clan (spelt 'Stewart' by the Scottish). He managed to keep many of the unruly lairds under control and to settle the **feuds** along the Borders, the area where Scotland joins England. For years both the Scottish and English had organized raids on each other across the Borders. James brought peace – known as 'King James's peace' – to the Borders region.

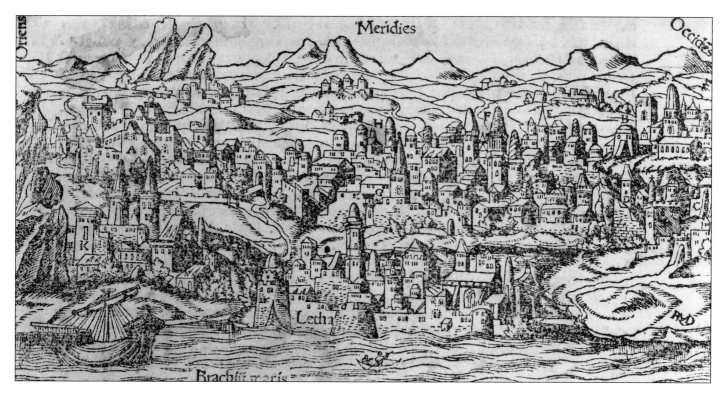

James had other successes, too. It was a time of religious change. Scotland and England had **converted** from the Catholic religion to the Protestant religion. James was head of the Protestant kirk (Scottish Church), but he worked hard to keep all the different religious groups happy.

James also helped Edinburgh grow into a wealthy, thriving city. He gave it a **charter**, and this led to the University of Edinburgh being set up. It was fitting that James should help the city to have a university because he was very well educated and liked to encourage the education of others.

(Above) A view of Edinburgh, James's birthplace. His court and the Scottish parliament were both in Edinburgh, and the city grew richer during his reign.

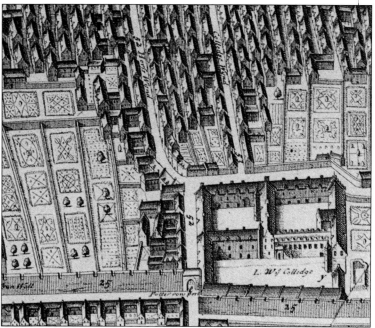

(Right) Edinburgh University during James's reign.

King of England

The year 1603 was a memorable one for James. It brought important news from England. Queen Elizabeth I, James's grandfather's cousin was dead – and she had no children. This meant that James was to become king of England. He was already James VI of Scotland, and now he would also become James I of England. This was exciting news, not only for James but for England and Scotland as well. At that time Scotland and England were two separate countries, and England had never had a Scottish king before.

James hoped to unite Scotland and England and give them one flag. These were some of the designs for it. The red cross on white is England's flag and the white cross on blue is Scotland's.

(Left) James and Anne's coronation at Westminster Abbey. The celebrations were cut short because of the **plague**, which was raging through London.

(Below) The red, white and blue jewel on James's chair was specially made to show the union of Scotland and England.

At first the English thought of James as a 'foreigner' because he spoke with a strong Scottish accent, which they were not used to. But most people welcomed him and looked forward to his reign.

After his coronation, James's dearest wish was to **unite** Scotland and England. He wanted them to become one country, Great Britain, with one kind of money and one flag. James asked the English **parliament** to agree to this. They said that they would look into it, but the two countries were not united during James's reign. Even so, James liked to call himself the king of Great Britain.

When James left Scotland in 1603, he promised to return every three years, but he only managed to go back once, in 1617.

On 5 November 1605, two years after James arrived in England, a group of Catholics decided to blow him up while he was opening Parliament. Guy Fawkes, a gunpowder expert, had been storing gunpowder under the Houses of Parliament in preparation. But an **anonymous** letter revealed the plot, and the day before Parliament's opening, the rooms underneath the building were searched. Guy Fawkes was discovered and arrested. Under torture, he signed a confession and was later executed, along with some of his fellow conspirators.

The lantern that Guy Fawkes used during the Gunpowder Plot.

It is likely that Catholics were unhappy because, during Henry VIII's reign, England had changed from a Catholic to a Protestant country. Catholics were often **persecuted** under Protestant rule. Although James was a Protestant, Catholics had hoped and believed that they would be treated better than they had been under Queen Elizabeth. This did happen, but they wanted more. Their disappointment may have led to the plot against King James.

King James I of England on horseback, with London in the background.

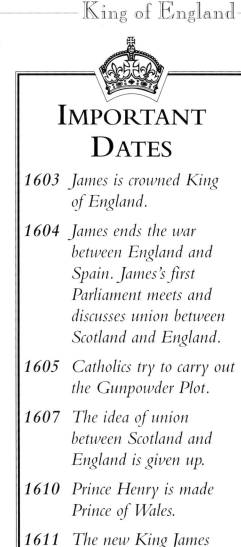

IMPORTANT DATES

1603 James is crowned King of England.

1604 James ends the war between England and Spain. James's first Parliament meets and discusses union between Scotland and England.

1605 Catholics try to carry out the Gunpowder Plot.

1607 The idea of union between Scotland and England is given up.

1610 Prince Henry is made Prince of Wales.

1611 The new King James Bible (or Authorized Version) is published.

1612 The death of Prince Henry.

Today, we remember the Gunpowder Plot every year on 5 November when we set off fireworks and burn a guy on a bonfire.

Guy Fawkes with his fellow conspirators. Some of them were killed as soon as they were captured; others were treated cruelly, then executed in public.

Prince Henry as a young boy. It was common for boys to wear dresses until around the age of five.

James's first child, Prince Henry, was nine years old when James travelled to England to become king. Father and son were very different from each other. James was peace-loving, while Henry loved everything to do with war. He enjoyed talking about wars and battles and going on long marches. Despite their differences, James was proud of Henry. He wanted to prepare his son for when he would become king, so he wrote a book for Henry called *Basilikon Doron*. It was full of advice about how to be a good ruler.

Unfortunately, Henry did not live long enough to put any of his father's advice into practice. He became ill when he was eighteen years old. Every type of medicine was tried. He was even given a substance called powdered unicorn's horn, but nothing helped and Henry died in 1612.

(Left) James sits on his throne, surrounded by his family. On his right are Queen Anne and Prince Henry. The skulls by their sides show that they had died when this was drawn. On James's left is his daughter Elizabeth with her husband and some of their thirteen children.

James's next eldest child was Elizabeth. She and Henry had been good friends, and he had often asked for her during his last illness. But she could not inherit the throne from her father because she was a girl and did not have the same rights as her brothers. So their younger brother Charles now stood next in line to the throne.

Princess Elizabeth, James's daughter. Shortly after her brother Henry's death, Elizabeth married and became Queen of Bohemia, which is now part of the Czech Republic.

While he lived in Scotland, James thought of England as a wealthy country. Now that he was the king of England, he was determined to live grandly. He and the queen surrounded themselves with courtiers – wealthy men and women who kept them company, advised them and looked after them.

This fine pair of embroidered leather gloves is thought to have belonged to James.

One of the most popular entertainments at **court** was the masque. This was a kind of play, with dancing, music and pantomime. Queen Anne employed the famous **playwright** Ben Jonson to write many of these masques. Inigo Jones, a famous **architect**, was paid to design the expensive sets and costumes. For one masque, Jones designed a huge float in the shape of a shell. This was drawn by seahorses, which seemed to be bobbing up and down

(Above) Queen Anne loved jewels. She wore them in her hair and had her clothes decorated with them.

on waves. In the centre sat Queen Anne, dressed in a jewelled gown and surrounded by attendants.

Many people thought it was wrong that the king and queen should spend so much money on things that were unimportant. One masque cost nearly £5,000 – a huge amount of money at that time.

This costume, sketched by Inigo Jones, was worn by Prince Henry at one of the many masques the queen gave at the royal court.

Life in England

ing James was often short of money. Apart from what he and the queen spent on masques, they spent lavishly on their children and on their home. They once bought two child beds (beds in which the queen gave birth) at a cost of £30,000.

James was also very generous to his friends. He often gave them money or expensive presents. In 1611 he gave £30,000 away, which today would be worth about £800,000. He could not afford to do this, and the result was that he often fell into **debt**.

IMPORTANT DATES

1614   *'Addled' Parliament meets. It was called 'addled' because it could not agree about anything and so no laws were passed.*

1619   *Queen Anne dies.*

1620   *The Mayflower carries the Pilgrim Fathers to America to set up the first New England* **colony**.

1624   *James's fourth and last Parliament meets to discuss possible war with Spain.*

1625   *James dies.*

Banqueting House in London. This building was designed by Inigo Jones, who designed many of the sets for Queen Anne's masques.

James was criticized by Parliament for spending too much time hunting and not enough time ruling his kingdom.

At times he could not pay his servants' wages, and so they would help themselves to some of the royal household goods, such as meat and drink, instead.

Whenever James ran into deep trouble, he would ask Parliament for help. Parliament could give him more money by increasing the taxes that ordinary people paid. But Parliament did not always do this because it disapproved of how James spent the money. Parliament was also unhappy about James's belief in the divine right of kings. This meant that James thought God brought kings and queens to power, and so only God – not Parliament – could question what the monarch did.

As James and his Parliament did not always agree, James only called Parliament together when he felt it was really necessary. In his twenty-two-year reign, Parliament met only four times.

James, seated in Parliament.

Throughout his life, James had his favourites. In Scotland, his favourite had been Esmé Stuart. In England, James drew a few more men into his circle.

One of these was Robert Carr, who was a good-looking, athletic young man but was not very clever. James first noticed him in 1607 at a **jousting tournament** in which Carr broke his leg. The king helped nurse Carr back to health and after that made him his companion. Much later, the relationship between the pair of them soured. Carr and his wife were imprisoned, accused of poisoning one of their friends. James eventually pardoned them and set them free. This was not a popular decision, and James was criticized for it.

A jousting tournament. It was at one of these events that James first met Robert Carr, one of his favourites.

A more worthy favourite was George Villiers, later Duke of Buckingham. James met this tall, handsome young man in 1614, when Carr was becoming unpopular. The king adored Villiers and so did the queen. She spoke of him affectionately as 'my kind dog', while James showered him and his family with gifts and titles. Villiers rose from being a knight to an earl, to a marquess and, finally, to a duke. He helped James in political matters. Later, when James was old and ill, Villiers and Charles, the king's son, took over much of the running of the country from the ageing king.

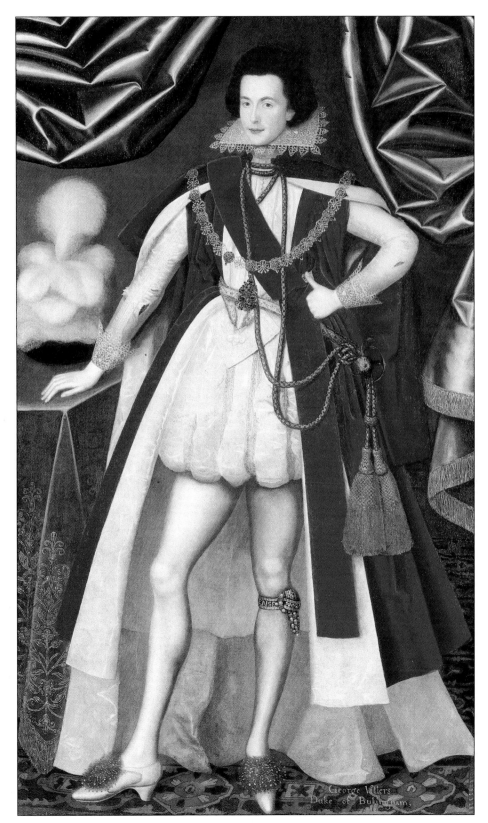

George Villiers, the Duke of Buckingham. James was very fond of him and kept a picture of him next to his heart.

(Above) James in old age, wearing the state robes. His motto, beati pacifici, is above his head. James worked hard to end the war between England and Spain and succeeded in 1604.

In 1625, when James was fifty-nine years old, he became ill. At first doctors thought that he would soon recover. However, he quickly grew worse and within three weeks he was dead. King James VI/I was buried in Westminster Abbey in London.

With the death of James, the **Jacobean period** was at an end. In the past, many people thought that James was a bad and foolish king and that the Jacobean period was not a good time in history. But people do not think this any more. James had many successes in his lifetime. One was the new translation of the Bible. James had found that only poor translations existed, so he appointed some **scholars** to work on a better one. In 1611 the new version, known as the King James Bible, or the Authorized Version, was published. This was so good that the Bible was not translated again for three hundred years.

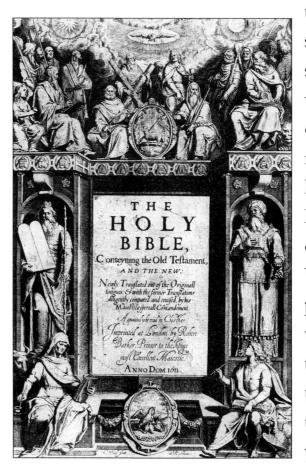

The opening page of the newly translated King James Bible. Arranging this translation was one of the king's great achievements.

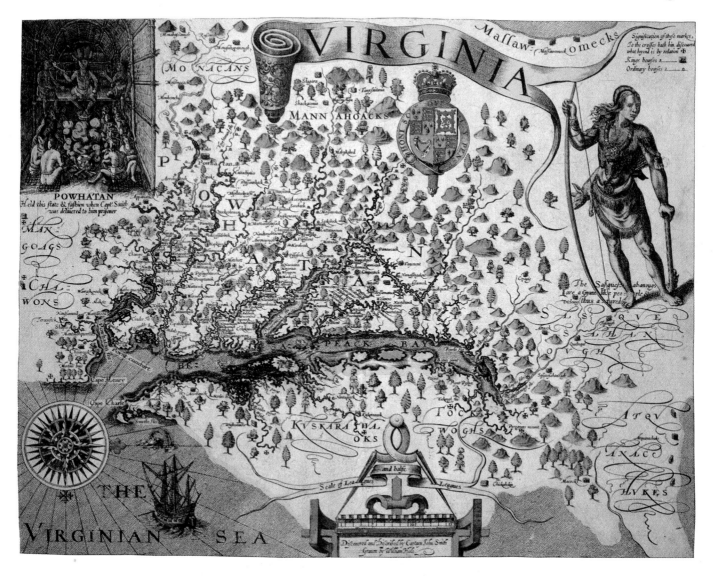

During King James's reign, England set up several colonies. In one of these, Virginia (in America), an English trader called John Smith was captured by Native Americans. They were angry with the English for taking over their land. Chief Powhatan, their leader, decided to put Smith to death. But his eleven-year-old daughter, Princess Pocahontas, pleaded for Smith's life and saved him.

After James's death, his son Charles became king of England. Charles I was an unpopular ruler and was beheaded in 1649.

A map of Virginia, one of England's colonies in America. Jamestowne, in the west, was named after King James. In the top left-hand corner is a picture of Chief Powhatan, drawn by John Smith.

Glossary

abdicate To give up being queen or king.

anonymous From a person who is unknown.

architect Someone who designs buildings.

Catholic A Christian who believes that the Pope is the Head of the Church.

charter A document giving special rights to a city.

colony A settlement in another country.

composition Writing exercises or essays that help a person learn to write well.

conspiracy A plot or plan, carried out in secret.

converted Changed.

coronation A ceremony to crown a king or queen.

court The royal household.

debt Owing money.

divine right of kings The idea that the right to be king or queen is given by God, and so no one but God can question what a king or queen does.

executed Killed.

feuds Quarrels.

governed Ruled.

interrogated Questioned.

Jacobean period The years when King James I ruled England, from 1603 to 1625. The word Jacobean comes from the Latin word for James, which is 'Jacobus'.

jousting tournament A sport in which people fight on horseback.

monarch A king, queen or emperor.

parliament The group of people who run a country.

persecuted Treated unfairly.

plague A serious disease that humans can catch from rats and that spreads rapidly.

playwright A person who writes plays.

Protestant A Christian who believes that the monarch is head of the Church.

regents People who rule in the place of a king or queen.

scholars People who are very clever and have studied hard.

Stone of Scone A sandstone block, with a Latin cross, which was traditionally present when a Scottish king was crowned.

translate To put something into another language.

tutor Teacher.

unite Join together.

Further Information

Books to Read

Gunpowder Plot by R. Nottridge (Wayland, 1991)
Spotlight on the Stuarts by S. Ross (Wayland, 1987)
Stuart Household by J. Ellenby (Cambridge University Press, 1981)
Stuarts by D. Bailey (Hodder & Stoughton, 1993)
The Stuarts by T. Wood (Paperbird, 1991)

Places to Visit

In Scotland:

Dunfermline Palace, Monastery Street, Dunfermline.
This royal palace was the birthplace of James's second son, Charles.

Edinburgh Castle, Castle Rock, Edinburgh.
James's birthplace and where he spent some of his adult life.

Falkland Palace, Falkland, Near Kirkcaldy, Fife.
Falkland Palace was built by James's grandfather and became the seat of the Scottish court. James went hunting nearby and was captured here during the Gowrie Conspiracy.

Huntingtower Castle, Near Perth.
Once known as Ruthven Castle, this is where the Raid of Ruthven took place.

Linlithgow Palace, South Shore of the Loch, Linlithgow, Near Edinburgh.
The birthplace of James's mother, Mary Queen of Scots.

Stirling Castle, Central Stirling.
James was baptized in the Chapel Royal, was crowned here and also spent the first thirteen years of his life here.

In England:

Banqueting House, Whitehall, London.
This was rebuilt in 1625 after a fire but contains ceiling paintings of James.

Westminster Abbey, Broad Sanctuary, London.
James and Anne's burial place.

Index

Figures in **bold** refer to illustrations. Glossary entries are shown by the letter g.